THE YEAR IS A CIRCLE

Victor Carl Friesen

Locale of the 76 Color Photographs:
(59 were taken in Saskatchewan; 36 of these
within 50 miles of Rosthern in mid-province)

Front cover - near Jasper, AB

frontispiece - Big Muddy Badlands, SK

opposite Contents - Meadow Lake Prov. Park, SK

The Year is a Circle

The Year is a Circle

A Celebration of Henry David Thoreau

Victor Carl Friesen

NATURAL HERITAGE / NATURAL HISTORY INC.

The Year is a Circle: A Celebration of Henry David Thoreau
by Victor Carl Friesen

Published by Natural Heritage / Natural History Inc.
P.O. Box 95, Station "O", Toronto, Ontario M4A 2M8

Design: Molly Brass
Printed and bound in Canada by Hignell Printing Limited,
Winnipeg, Manitoba

Canadian Cataloguing in Publication Data

Friesen, Victor Carl
The year is a circle: a celebration of Henry David Thoreau

Includes text by Henry David Thoreau.
ISBN 1-896219-03-9

1. Thoreau, Henry David, 1817-1862 – Knowledge – Natural history.
2. Nature in literature.   3. Nature – Pictorial works. I . Thoreau, Henry
David, 1817-1862. II Title.

PS3057.N3F75 1995   818'.309

Natural Heritage / Natural History Inc. gratefully
acknowledges the assistance of the Canada Council, the Ontario Arts
Council, and the Government of Ontario through the Ministry
of Citizenship, Tourism and Recreation.

For Dorothy

Contents

Photographs

Preface

HENRY DAVID THOREAU is internationally known for his classic book, *Walden,* 1854, in which he described his simple life living in a hut beside Walden Pond near Concord, Massachusetts. This was only a two-year sojourn, but his whole life was spent close to the natural world, including his Yankee excursion into Canada, for he wrote in *Walden* that "we can never have enough of nature." In the fourteen volumes of his published journal, he wrote in similar vein. In an early volume he says, "I love the landscape," and in the last volume he continues: "expressions of our delight which any natural object draws from us are something complete and final in themselves."

The poems and photographs in this book are expressions of such love of landscape, in tribute to Thoreau. They are not attempts to describe a specific incident in his life; nor do they, for the most part, stem from a specific passage of his writings. Rather, they have for their inspiration the very thing that inspired the Concord saunterer – nature itself: he ever approached it with sensuousness and childlike wonder. Of course, since I am a long-time student of Thoreau, the influence of this mentor can be readily seen – perhaps in phrase or thought, certainly in the flavor or atmosphere of the poetry and photographs.

The poetry is typically traditional, mostly blank verse, in keeping with the times of this nineteenth-century naturalist. Largely descriptive, the poems collectively reinforce Thoreau's repeated notion that the year is a circle. The photographs are not directly illustrative of the poetry, although a few words from each poem serve as captions. The pictures were selected to complement the poetry in leaving sensuous impressions and tend to focus on what is universal in nature, experienced in a variety of outdoor locales. They were taken in both Canada and the United States, but chiefly in my home province of Saskatchewan, a region removed from Thoreau's native New England. Doing so was really not inappropriate, for in his first book, *A Week on the Concord and Merrimack Rivers*, 1849, Thoreau states that "Nature is one and continuous everywhere." Indeed, his ecological concerns know no national boundaries.

What is depicted, then – described by words or evoked through illustration – are Thoreau-like experiences through the cycle of the day from dawn to nightfall, through the months and seasons of the year, ending with the triumph of spring as in *Walden*. A short passage or two from Thoreau's writings, which touch on the experience, serve as an epigraph for each poem. (These passages are from *The Writings of Henry David Thoreau*, 20 vols., Walden edn., Boston: Houghton Mifflin, 1906. The journal forms Vols. VII-XX, which is also numbered *Journal* I-XIV. The quotations above, in order, are from *Walden*, II, 35; *Journal*, II, 100 and XIV, 117; and *Week*, I, 372. The book's title is from *Journal*, III, 438.)

Some of the poems have appeared previously in *Blue Jay* and *Thoreau Journal Quarterly*, and the introductory poem appeared also in my critical study of Thoreau's sensuous approach to nature, *The Spirit of the Huckleberry*, 1984.

Victor Carl Friesen

Thoreau

HENRY DAVID THOREAU lived almost all of his short life in Concord, Massachusetts. He was born in this rural New England town in 1817 and died there, of tuberculosis, in 1862. His life as a writer had far-reaching results, not only in his own country but world-wide.

His works are now studied in any survey of American literature – who has not heard about marching to "a different drummer," for instance (*Walden*, II, 358)? In the natural sciences, he is looked upon as America's greatest nature writer as well as a pioneer in ecology. *Walden* and his other books and essays reveal his ear for the music of nature, and the thousands of pages of his daily journal have become a valuable mine of information. In the social sciences, he has at least a double appeal. With his essay on "Resistance to Civil Government" (he aided slaves escaping to Canada), he influenced Mahatma Gandhi in achieving India's independence. Economically, he advocated a simple life – so that one could be "extravagant" in harvesting sensations from the natural world: "Superfluous wealth can buy superfluities only" (*Walden*, II, 363). Today, the Thoreau Society, an international organization of students and admirers of Thoreau, includes members in more than twenty countries.

How is it that a life of but forty-four years could be so productive? Thoreau liked to say that he was "born in the most estimable place in all the world, and in the very nick of time, too" (*Journal*, III, 160). Among his close friends right in Concord were Ralph Waldo Emerson, Nathaniel Hawthorne, and educator Bronson Alcott. Louisa May, Alcott's daughter and, later, author of *Little Women*, was, in fact, Thoreau's pupil when, for three years, he ran a private elementary school after graduating from Harvard. Thereafter, he took up land surveying, pencil making (he devised various techniques to improve the product), and doing odd jobs of manual labor. These provided him both sufficient income and time to saunter, to reflect, and to write. That his collected works number twenty volumes speaks for his industry. (Princeton University Press is now publishing, over a period of years, a new edition of his writings.)

Thoreau always wanted "to live deliberately, to front only the essential facts of life, and see if [he] could not learn what it had to teach, and not, when [he] came to die, discover that

[he] had not lived" (*Walden*, II, 100-101). If at times his often humorously stated ideas on life and society seem radical, they may also be considered a "sublime conservatism" (his term) (*Week*, I, 140), a principled, unwavering adherence to a higher law. Emerson had said that one should hitch one's wagon to a star. Thoreau optimistically did. He built his castles in the air, but down-to-earth Yankee that he was, then put foundations under them – an approach he recommended for everyone. He believed that reform must start with the individual self, and to be a philosopher, he said, required that the problems of living be solved, not merely theoretically, but practically.

The observations of this naturalist-philosopher remain as pertinent in our time as when he first made them:

> "Only that day dawns to which we are awake" (*Walden*, II, 367).

> "Our inventions…are but improved means to an unimproved end" (*Walden*, II, 58).

> "In Wildness is the preservation of the World" ("Walking," V, 224).

Succeeding generations will continue to find something new and meaningful in the rich heritage of his writings.

Introduction

....

"The day is an epitome of the year. The night is
the winter, the morning and evening are the
spring and fall, and the noon is the summer."

(*Walden*, II, 332)

1

"…there lay the transparent pond already calm and full of hope as in a summer evening"; "…it was morning, and lo, now it is evening"; "…waiting at evening on the hill-tops for the sky to fall, that I might catch something."

(*Walden*, II, 344, 124, 19)

At Walden Pond

This is my pond, not mine to own but mine
To know the greatness of – to see the chill,
Gray ghost of dawn evolving from the water,
Or so it seems, and then the sunlit fog
Has curled its vapors from my sight: the pond
Lies new and silver-blue, shaking the sun's
Light in my face.

               Was that the loon's loud laugh,
Or was the wilderness once crying out
To me? Sometimes I hear, but I don't know
What I have heard (my thoughts were far away),
And then my mind rings clear – but not enough;
Perhaps there is a sound in silence too.
Yet never mind – the pond is fashioned from
The dawn into the day; ducks dive in depths

Of ooze and quack contentedly. I listen –
But there's too much to hear, to hear a thing.

This is my pond, not mine to slip the sleek
Fish from, though I do that at times. The line
I use seems but a cord that fixes me
To nature. Such a tie needs careful tending,
Or the small hold it has may loose itself
And at some superficial joy let go
The small hold altogether.

              Slowly now
The day fades into night – and soon the pond
In evening lies, a breadth of burnished fire
With scattered flames against the sky in gold
And green and mauve. And then the gold is gone,
And silver-calm and silhouette have come:
My pond now has more beauty than I see
With mortal eyes. A still merganser slides
His glassy way to sheltered rest – so I
To mine, though I would gladly stay and wait.

"the chill, / Gray ghost of dawn"

"shaking the sun's / Light"

"fashioned from / The dawn into the day"

"the pond / In evening lies"

Seasons

"There is a season for everything, and we do not notice a given phenomenon except at that season, if, indeed, it can be called the same phenomenon at any other season. There is a time to watch the ripples on Ripple Lake, to look for arrowheads, to study the rocks and lichens, a time to walk on sandy deserts; and the observer of nature must improve these seasons as much as the farmer his.... The moods and thoughts of man are revolving just as steadily and incessantly as nature's."

(*Journal*, XII, 159)

Summer

....

*"…we inhaled the fresh scent of every field,
and all nature lay passive, to be viewed and
travelled"; "Our eyes rested on…skies of
Nature's painting."*

("A Walk to Wachusett," V, 136, 144)

Summer Days

....

There is but one sure season in our hearts
Through all the year's swift circle – that is summer.
The urgent vibrancy of spring is its
Brief preface (just as fall which follows is
Its gold fruition, and then winter yet
Another summer, waiting, safe beneath
The snow).

       Once summertime has fully come,
The days grow languid, slow their pace, with each
Succeeding day a copy of the one
Before it: skies, cerulean in hue,
Are softly packed with raft-like clouds adrift
In space, their molded tops now showy with
A blue-white opalescence; meadows, low
Beneath the overwhelming sky, stretch out
In undulating slopes and hollows, green
With waving grasses, bright with flowers of
Midsummer – silverweed and creamy yarrow,
Red prickly rose and purple blazing-star.

The many-scented meadows seem alive
With sweet sensation, movement, as each blade
Of grass, each blossom, sways, and as the clouds
Above them slip their far-flung shadows through
The verdant growth. Atop the reedy grass,
A restive bobolink, in black and white
Display, casts off to mount aslant into
The suddenly expectant air, while from
Its teeming throat spills out, in liquid notes,
Such melody, a spontaneity
Of bursting, circling sound – until the song's
Diminished as the bird descends to earth.

The meadow lies in silence, greater than
Before, and all the land and sky bespeak
To us the immobility of things
Once summer has come round – the flowers and
The grass, for all their waving, still are seen
To be fast-rooted where they were; above,
The sky's still filled with downy clouds,
Still drifting on, still changing, ever changeless:
The season's enterprise is fixing on
The slowly turning hub of wheeling time.

So the warm, golden light which shines at last
At each day's close is caught by tops of clouds
High-pillared in the east, reflecting light
From sunny daytime's realm, a copper sheen
Upon the waving grass and flowers, and
Extending the glad presence of each day,
Anticipating further sunny hours,
Which wait behind the earth's great curvature.

"the days grow languid"

"softly packed with raft-like clouds"

"atop the reedy grass"

"sunny daytime's realm"

June

"As I walked along close to the edge of the water, the sea…flow[ed] with a flat white foaming edge and a rounded outline up the sand."

~ June 19, 1857 (*Journal*, IX, 443)

On Cape Cod

....

The opaque moon,
Probing with tentacle beams
Twilight's ethereality,
Rises from the cold sea water
To haunt the pivoting fish
Suspended there
Above the sand-covered clam bed,
The sandy pasture where the starfish feed.

Wee-ee-loo-oo-oo,
The upland plover cries.
Wee-loo-oo,
Across the water
Chucking the headland
Sounds the plaintive cry.

As ever, I look out to sea,
To landlessness,
The genesis of my well-being
And confrontation with my primal self.
Standing here, I know
The wind I bend against
This evening by the sea
(And the wind smells of the sea –
Odorous it is of scavenged crabs
And lime-encrusted stones
And kelp
And clean white salt).

I know the sea…
Rushing up the land
In one expansive foaming edge,
Idly fingering pebbles within reach –
All resistless
In its grating undulation –
And slipping down the shore.

Hold fast or come again,
Hold fast or come again:
Ocean – moonlit, salty, cold;
Poet – knowing the sea, hearing the cry…

"twilight's ethereality"

"to landlessness"

"genesis of my well-being"

"its grating undulation"

July

"There is something serenely glorious and memorable to me in the sight of the first cool sunlight now gilding the eastern extremity of the bushy island in Fair Haven, that wild lake."

~ July 4, 1852 (*Journal*, IV, 181)

Shore Morning

At a northern lake
In the misty wake
Of dawn,
I yawn
And splash cold water into my eyes.
The sun soon comes up past the black rise
Of the shore, and I know morning's here:
The great lake is steel-blue, still and clear.

Watching the sunlight
Catching the trees night
Has held in darkness, I stand
Upon the gravelly strand
In joyous expectation –
And in my exultation

I launch my canoe
Into the cold blue
And whip it away from shore.
Then resting my paddle once more,
I listen…
I listen…

A kingfisher splashes –
His brilliant coat flashes
A metallic fire in spray;
While beyond, over the bay,
A white tern soundlessly rows the blue sky
With cleaving wings: then stops short – in its eye
A surfacing fish. The bird
Flutters – I say not a word –
Then collapses –
Plopses! plapses! –
The circling waves well out from the dive.

Now I'm paddling ahead to arrive
At the point in the bay,
On this summer-glad day,
Where two islands lie, thatched
With pine forests and matched
In enchantment, and one I choose
Where I beach my canoe. My shoes

Soon are treading,
Soon are shedding,
The rippled white sand. To perfection
The shore juts above its reflection.

Up from the beach the pines
Form corridors with lines
Of solid trunks, a scented stillness where
The smell of last year's leaves is in the air:
I walk across
Lichens and moss
And see the blue lake through the trees.
The branches soon stir with a breeze
Starting up – the lake has been
Dappled with sunlight – but in
My retreat the soft shadows hold sway.

And I lay me back this summer's day,
With my head in the cup
Of my hands, looking up
From grass that is sweet, soft, and cool.
A cloud floats along in its pool
Of sky,
While I
Can sleepily dream,
Can sleepily dream.

"steel-blue, still and clear"

"a scented stillness"

"soft shadows hold sway"

"a cloud floats along"

August

"[I] [s]ee a large hen-hawk sailing…, soaring at last very high and toward the north. At last it returns southward…, without apparent motion. It thus moves half a mile directly."

~ August 25, 1860 (*Journal*, XIV, 61)

On Fair Haven Hill

My feet aren't tired of long standing in
A single spot. Early today they brought
Me to this shadow-lake of coolness here
Beside some poplars on a hill – here where
The dew is seeded on each curve of grass
Or dropped within each flower's throat, and mint
Leaves crushed are aromatic like some spruce
Woods lived in, in my dreams. And so I stand
Immersed in nature's world at noon: it seems
It's just another tree that I've become,
Moveless, watching the moted sunlight drift
Among the frieze-like spaces held within
The season's verdure. Burning is the sun

Which gilds those leaves of summer-green, and dark
Against the gold a silhouetted few
Still flutter. Yet enveloped in the moist,
Sweet exhalation of the shaded earth,
I am a cool and quiet center of
The heat-blurred land about me.

                           It is then
My eyes first see a naked branch, a perch
For birds, and clutching talons deep into
This limb, three silent hawks sit sentinel –
A trio predatory, proudly sure.
Six eyes have fixed me with their stony gaze
(The tails flick back and forth uneasily),
Six wings extend akimbo, waiting,…till
The branch dips down three times as one great hawk
Springs to the east and one swoops west and a
Reluctant, slower third soars northward. Soon,
They wheel above my head, directing down
Their screaming arrows, claiming prior right
To branch and tree, to sunlit hill and sky.
And searing is the sun's pervading light
To eyes held upward, as on they sail. High
And circling higher, faring farther than
The tallest tree, they gather, caught within

The shining whiteness of a cloud: lonely
Now all the land in torpid heat below.

The hawks, with other realms to rule, swing wide,
Away from wind-torn clouds above to where
The far horizon yields in compact mass
A line advancing – milky summits huge
And growing huger, bottoms dark with rain
To slake what is abnormal midday heat.
The birds – they've disappeared against the sky.

And now a sudden gusty wind begins
To ripple grass about my feet; one small
Blue flower starts its nodding in the grass
That's rippling. Strange, I should be standing yet
Upon this lonely spot without my giving
A second thought to tired feet. And strange,
On turning homeward, trampling grass from which
The light once glinted, only then I feel
How close to being rooted in the earth
My feet have been: I pick up heavy feet
In walking briskly, watching storm clouds come.
My feet are leaden, but my heart is light.

"exhalation of the shaded earth"

"a line advancing – milky summits"

"watching storm clouds come"

Autumn

"I think that the change to some higher color in a leaf is an evidence that it has arrived at a late and perfect maturity, answering to the maturity of fruits"; "As fruits and leaves and the day itself acquire a bright tint just before they fall, so the year near its setting."

("Autumnal Tints," V, 250, 251)

Autumn Afternoon

On this late sunny afternoon, I hear
The cricket's skirling still, an undertone
In Gaelic mode, a singing in the air,
Which, were it not to be, the earth had lost
Its music. Sere brown is the color of
The sound, made mellow through the distances
Of golden haze transcribing it.

                                               These are
Rich autumn days – maples luxuriant
As ripened fruit, each tree a scarlet globe,
Full of red juices in each leaf; elm trees
Here drooping weighted limbs of foliage,
Like rounded yellow marrows warming in
The sun. Above, the cope of sky is blued
Its deepest hue, lustrous corolla for
The calyx-earth. For every part of this
Fall scene is flower: grasses bent and filled
With crickets' humming, trees that glow within
As slow-maturing fruit, a sky startling
In blueness – such is the abundance of
All color. Even russet brush, bereft

Of summer's roses, palely gleams amid
Near hills, and farther hills have purplish casts
From smoke of far-off fires.

                        Across the whole,
Wide, intervening space, the ending day
Is hushed (the color ever vibrant to
The eye, the silence almost audible) –
Only the twittering of vireos
In passage, scattered in a hedge; the rush
Of wings from crows in streams of silent flight,
Seeking their evening roost; and skirling sound
Which wells, it seems, from earth, amalgam of
Sensations, music of the autumn lands.

"red juices in each leaf"

"weighted limbs of foliage"

"amalgam of / Sensations"

September

"At sundown McCauslin pointed over the forest…to signs of fair weather amid the clouds, – some evening redness there."

~ September 3, 1846 (*The Maine Woods*, III, 28)

In the Maine Woods

Evening;
The sweep of northern sky;
The shower-ruined vesture of a cloud,
Lurid in the sunset:
Gilded crimson, flaming orange, and lambent yellow;
A golden prolongation;
A breath withheld;
Then soundless death
Of burnished bronze and mauve and Indian red;
A silent land beneath a silent sky –
With distant birds like small black stars,
And trees in ageless amber.
A white-throat's sudden song
Embroiders the great silence with a silken frill.

A man sits at his cabin door and takes
His ease. In thoughts unmeasured he recounts
His daytime prose: the fourteen trees he chopped
To build a pen for his one pig (the axe
Now leans within his reach), the branches cut
And piled to feed his stove when they are dry,
The sod potatoes that he dug, the cow
That overturned his pail at milking time.
He sees the shapeless barn, a square of logs
Roofed with a mound of graying, musty hay;
The brindle cow abed before the smudge,
Content, chewing her cud, her head within
The smoke; the horse that stands with drooping head –
One leg held limp – and bears her company;
The spotted calf that frisks about the yard
And then stops short before the unconcerned,
Contented cow. Beyond the yard he sees
The scattered stumps, the chips of wood that mark
His next year's field; and then the bulking gloom
Of forest – poplar, alder, and black spruce –
With which he must contend for space to live.
He pictures how the field will look next fall,
And thinks about the loads of scented hay
He'll stack and then haul home. He sees within
His mind another cow, a better barn,
A garden with more room. He wonders if
A frost this year might harm the melons and
The beans, if he should build a snake fence for

His stock, and if the brindle cow will not
Go dry ere winter come. He glances at
The sky for signs of rain, breathes deeply of
The damp night air that's tinged with brushwood smoke,
And feels the grass for dew. This done, he steps
Into his hut, shuts out the night, and lights
His coal-oil lamp. He sets his supper things
Aside, fills up his pipe, and reaching for
A book of old romance, he sits and reads.
Without, the poetry of night goes on.

Darkness;
A mothy stillness;
The mellowed orange of a new-rising moon,
Half-hidden in the spruce tops;
Its slow progression through pellucid space,
Higher, higher –
(The soughing wind within the trees,
The far-off hooting of an owl) –
Then the clearing sealed in moon-enchantment:
The magic ruins of a barn;
A cabin palely washed in a strange splendor;
Stumps standing in their pools of shadow;
Strewn, whitened chips;
The encircling woods with branches tipped with light.
The unseen owl hoots once, is still;
The wind has hushed;
The clearing sleeps beneath the peaceful moon.

"the shower-ruined vesture of a cloud"

"golden prolongation; / A breath withheld"

"the bulking gloom / Of forest"

"the encircling woods"

October

"There were the tawny rocks…defying the ocean, whose waves incessantly dashed against and scoured them with vast quantities of gravel."

~ October 9, 1849 (*Cape Cod*, IV, 17)

A Stroll upon the Beach

It's brewing up a storm, no doubt. Out far,
The ocean froths and spills upon itself
As water in a pail might do when swung
About one's head (as farm boys home from school
Have swung) and then stopped short. The water's dark
And heavy like the leaden sky, hiding
Some somber mystery within its green
And suffocating depths. Above, the clouds,
In roiling disarray, scud north and then
Are piled in overlapping rows where sea
And sky form one blurred line. I know somewhere
It's raining, for the smell is heavy on
The air. But here the darkest night creeps in,
Now pausing imperceptively; now at

A sudden pounce, obliterating all
The storm and its wild tossing, only save
The roar, the crashing roar of wave on wave.

Tomorrow, when the ocean settles somewhat,
Beneath the cloud mass, thick and gray, I'll stroll
The gravel beach (the wind is but a brisk
Sea breeze and salt upon my lips). And where
A drift log's foiled the ocean's sudden wrath
By stowing treasure on its landward side,
I'll crouch to probe the water-heavy sand,
And cupping fragments with cupped hand, I'll find
A broken keyhole and a red sea-star.

"froths and spills upon itself"

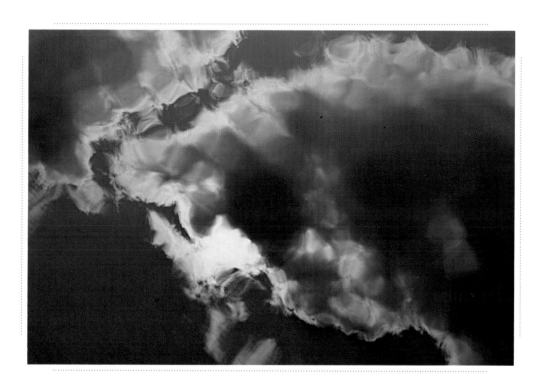

"clouds, / In roiling disarray"

"the wind is but a brisk / Sea breeze"

"treasure on its landward side"

November

"And what shall we name the faint aurora that precedes the moonrise?"

~ November 12, 1851 (*Journal*, III, 109)

Moon Rising

I wandered up the hill to see the moon,
New-risen, saffron-orange through the stand
Of trees before it; and above the trees
The sky was luminescent apple-green
In imitation of the later night's
Aurora; at my feet the dew-wet grass
Was silvered with wan light, while weed stalks drooped
In shadow. Giving voice to the night world
Were the who-whoing of a distant owl
And all about me crickets' shrilling: one,
Primeval in its tone, mysterious,
Implying darkened woods and wilderness;
The other, homely, rural in its strain,
Incessant, and bespeaking meadowlands.

Why this incessant strain of earth-music –
This muffled hooting from the darkened woods –
These chanticleers of a slow-rising moon?
One would have thought the moon was sight enough
Without the need for sound, the dome of night
Should stretch from horizontal arc to arc
And not be echo chamber for a bird
Or bird-like cricket. But whatever was
The heralding, the moon, unheeding, moved
In space; in unrelenting progress, slipped
From branch to slow-releasing blackened branch,
Foiling the strength of the night-twisted trees,
As higher, ever higher, gaining might
And luster, it at last came free – new, chill,
Bright coinage of the sky, the world below
In silver light – and I heard not a sound.

"weed stalks drooped /In shadow"

"all about me crickets' shrilling"

"darkened woods and wilderness"

"bright coinage of the sky"

Winter

....

"…a few straggling snowflakes are beginning
to descend. Faster and faster they fall, shutting
out distant objects from sight"; "…see how the
silvery dust lies on every seared leaf and twig,
deposited in such infinite and luxurious forms
as by their very variety atone for the absence
of color."

("A Winter Walk," V, 181, 169)

Winter's Onset

The world's become an unremitting gray:
The winter sky opaque without a hint
Of color – and its upward bending arch,
In paradox, a low and seeming flat
Impasto, out of which a few small flakes
Descend in grayish whirls. Above, the snow
Is dark against the zenith, but before
The leaden rim of sky, the falling flakes
Look light. With parallel and slantwise strokes
They cut right through the circling edge of earth
And blend the sky to land. The snowy fields
Extend their textured slopes of gray on gray
(Eroded by continual ground-drift)
To blurred horizons. Were there not some light
That's filtered through the overcast and caught
By sculptured surfaces, the distant fields
Would show no meeting line with somber sky;
And bushes, leafless, streaked with falling snow,
Would seem to float in space, small islands of
A darker gray, now rooted in the air
And motionless in winter's monochrome.

"an unremitting gray"

"without a hint / Of color"

"caught / By sculptured surfaces"

"winter's monochrome"

December

"The strong wind from the north blows the snow almost horizontally, and, beside freezing you, almost takes your breath away."

~ December 29, 1853 (*Journal*, VI, 32)

Merry Blizzard

Up high, the storm is raging –
It's Mother Nature's glee;
She sweeps the snow from the heaven's floor
And puffs and pants, does she.

"A merry blizzard's coming,"
The lusty woman shrieks;
The snow comes thick and the wind blows hard,
And cold bites at our cheeks.

The maple trees bend downward,
Their branches fling about,
Like grayish wraiths from an olden time
In some vague dance, no doubt.

The world's soon one of whiteness –
The old dame's seen to that;
Frayed tufts of grass and odd blocks and stumps
Are hummocks round and fat.

The birds have gone to shelter
In spruce trees draped with snow;
A droop-winged robin there swells his breast
And chirrups once for show.

And I dress at his calling –
I must be outdoors too –
To wade and flounder in all the drifts
And feel the cold right through.

Then hail to wintry weather,
The best time of the year;
To wind and snow and the biting cold,
To grandame raise a cheer.

"frayed tufts of grass"

"the birds have gone to shelter"

"to wade and flounder in"

"hail to wintry weather"

January

"Standing thus on one side of the hill, I begin to see a pink light reflected from the snow there about fifteen minutes before the sun sets. This gradually deepens to purple and violet."

~ January 10, 1859 (*Journal*, XI, 395)

Winter Blue

Blue slopes of drifted snow reflect the sky
As twilight yields to the swift coming on
Of winter's night. A cold and opaque plain
Of blueness, whitish-blue, extends to where
The sky, an amethystine web, curves down
To meet it. In the east the lowering,
Round sweep of sky would almost seem to be
Portending onset of a storm – such is
The earnestness of nightfall there – were not
The brooding azured depths devoid of cloud –
Clear, pure, and continent.

The western sky,
In counterpoise, is filled with subdued light –
A purplish tint descending from the heights,
Then fading to mild rose with satiny
Appearance, then to tawny-rose along
The skyline, pallid dusky orange, which
Now complements the sloping western fields
Whose bluishness is shot with rosy sheen
For one brief moment in the changing light.

The colors deepen in the west, and this
Sky too grows dark – as does the drifted snow.
Blue snow becoming bluer, deeper blue,
And darker – indigo and finally
A violet that shades into an all
Absorbing black in far recesses. But
The snowy reaches of the earth maintain
A blueness, seen at last by starlight, pale
Beneath the velvet of the star-filled sky.

"blue slopes of drifted snow"

"plain / Of blueness, whitish-blue"

"clear, pure, and continent"

February

"Then there is the wonderful stillness of a winter day. The sources of sound…are frozen up; scarcely a tinkling rill of it is to be heard…. It is the Sabbath of the year."
~ February 13, 1859 (*Journal*, XI, 446)

A Winter Walk

All night, as we were soundly sleeping, then
The air was yet alive with falling snow,
Large flake on flake descending, feathering
The earth with whiteness. When the gray dawn came,
The snow lay thick on roof and window ledge,
Upon the axe, embedded in a stump,
And on its slanting handle – every stump
Nearby wore its own tippet of white down.
In time the eastern sky grew rose, this still
Before the sun had risen, and in turn
Each partly frosted window pane was tinged
With bluish-rose within its glaze of ice.

On opening the door and stepping out
Beyond the rounded stalactite of snow
That curved down from the eaves, I stopped – and was

Enveloped by a silent world: nothing
Was stirring, everything immovable
Beneath the snowy cover, creatures of
The wild now gone to earth; no creaking trees
To right or left, only the drooping spruce
Or bare-limbed, upright poplar; and behind
Me just the soundless, curling smoke (a tinge
Of rose and bluish color too) of my
Own chimney, rising ever upward in
Its unimpeded exploration of
The sky.

      Well-dressed, I strode into this strange
And silent world, crunching the powder-snow
With swinging steps, feeling the cold, dry air
About my face and stinging in my nostrils.
At length the sun arose amid the far
Horizon's frosty haze, blue shadowings
Appearing on bleak winter's sculpted slopes.
The scattered farms were now behind me, and
My view was shielded by surrounding hills
And bushes – not at all the slightest glimpse
Of any habitation.

      Here I stopped
To give my thoughts full play – where was I, thus
Enclosed within an eggshell whiteness? Was

The place the wilds of Labrador or perhaps
Some far-off Rupert's Land? Was I but some
Black speck amid the vast and snowy plains
Stretching indifferently from me? – or
A self-assured lone trapper breaking trail
Across the wilds? My mind delved deeper – how?
When? – why? – the very stuff of metaphysics.
For answer, nature was as silent as
Before when I had paused at my own door.
I let my eye sweep round the circle of
The whole horizon's rim – just silent plains
Of pale blue snow as they had been before,
Edged here and there with stands of grayish trees,
Nothing astir in seemingly a cold
And sterile world. I simply stood with all
Of nature yet expressionless before
Me.

      Then there came a flurry of small wings:
Alighting near me was a restive flock
Of tiny birds with tiny legs and feet,
Now twittering amid the snow, about
Some stark, dried weeds and weed-seeds lying there.
Half-fluttering, they hopped between the stalks
And left a maze of tracks (the writing of
Primeval nature in the snow), then clung

Onto the tops of dipping, swaying weeds
Like some new kind of winter flower – such
The lively, social feeding of these birds.
Redpolls they were, each with its forehead spot
Of darkest crimson, scarcely showing in
Their rare disport among the weed stalks. So
They flourished for a moment, cheering in
This short encounter. Yet one of the birds
I had not noticed, when it turned itself
Full towards me – startling, glowing, was its color,
A breast splashed with a brighter crimson, there
Exuding warmth for all the season, bird
Of paradise in barren winter, bold
And hardy in the snow.

              And then as at
Some secret password, every bird sprang up
In flight, each bird in fluid motion with
Its fellow, animated by one mind.
The flock whirled once with jingling notes and sweep
Of wings, whirled yet again, and flowed away
From view. Left in my mind were pictures still
Of tiny birds in lively sport, of one
Bird's dazzling warmth in sternest winter time:
Nature had asked no question of me then,
Nor answered none, I knew, nor had it need.

"its own tippet of white down"

"enveloped by a silent world"

"enclosed within an eggshell whiteness"

"in sternest winter time"

Spring

"*The first flock of geese is seen beating to north,
in long harrows and waving lines*"; "*Surely joy
is the condition of life.*"

("Natural History of Massachusetts,"
V, 110, 106)

Spring's Coming

The snow is barely gone, gray drifts of it,
Compressed to ice, still lying cold upon
The frozen ground beneath (where shade
Persists) – and then a gentle rain comes down,
The first of the spring season's showers: soft
Its fall upon the sodden earth, upon
The matted grasses, bleached but redolent
Of springtime odors, mix of damp decay
And fresh green growth. Already hillsides show
A delicate, pale greenish cast, washed as
They are of winter's refuse. Myriad
Young blades of grass are there; pervading all
An elemental tenderness; the year,
With one small flower open, now come round
Again.

      A distant robin sits upon
A dripping twig and carols of the rain,
The slowly greening hills, and of the long
Spring evening coming on (and also of
The line of amber in the clearing west).

A chilly dusk descends at last, with yet
Some sleety rain, and somewhere over woods
Too dark to see, some honking geese fly low,
Driving, their wings a-rush, into the sure
Retreat of winter when it must be spring.

"the snow is barely gone"

"where shade / Persists"

"matted grasses, bleached"

"retreat of winter when it must be spring"

March

"Now, then, spring is beginning again in earnest after this short check…. Is there not always an early promise of spring…followed by a short return of winter?… All nature is thus forward to move with the revolution of the seasons."
~ March 17, 1853 (*Journal*, V, 22-23)

Early Spring

An open hayfield, pale with evening's close;
Gray, somber clouds, banked in the far northwest,
Unmoving, ominous; a feline wind,
Now playing, icy-clawed, with tufts of grass,
Now pausing in capricious mood, about
To pillage the expected stillness of
The coming night; an ineffectual moon,
Blue-white in the illusive light of dusk;
A solemn crow, its perch half-mast within
A tree; a brooding tension in the air.
The clouds, wind, moon, and the black bird, austere –
Portending terse denial of the spring?
Forecasting winter's cold renewal?

Then,
A quick expectancy (the world is one),
A statement given: seven tundra swans
Now winging, swift, into the northern night
In changeless pattern, silent, restless, free,
And crying a white triumph from the sky.

"pale with evening's close"

"stillness of / The coming night"

"the illusive light of dusk"

"a brooding tension in the air"

April

*"It was remarkable how much light those white gulls…absorbed and reflected through
the sombre atmosphere, — conspicuous almost as candles in the night. When we got
near the gulls, they rose heavily and flapped away."*

~ April 15, 1855 (*Journal*, VII, 310-311)

To Great Meadows

The man and his companion briskly strode
The muddied pathway, leading down among
The scrubby hills though scattered birch and poplar.
The flooded meadows were before them then.
Low-lying hills and shoreline opposite
Now had a bluish misty tinge, the clumps
Of intervening shrubs a haze of green.
Each stepped onto a knoll, with nothing said,
And stood on tiptoe, gaining vantage there
To glimpse the sweep of water through the trees.

It still was not a time to talk but just
To look, to watch the meadow river's broad
And fluid surface changing constantly,
Its flows outridden and enveloped by
Still others; slicks of water moving to,
And lost in meeting, rippled portions – all
Sliding forward ceaselessly.

                    Out along
The shoreline where a spit of sand curved round
To form a bay, half-hidden by a screen
Of bushes, seven gulls stood lined up for
Inspection, everyone immaculate
In plumage, white of breast with pearl-gray wings.
The man and his companion did not move
But waited, watching…just a row of gulls
Whose forms were clean and pure against the brown
And greenish river rushing by. And then,
As if at some one moment pre-arranged,
The gulls arced out their graceful wings and one
By one in winnowed flight gained lift-off from
The sandbar, drifting on to either side,
Still low above the water. Mirror-like,
The surface caught each gull, developing
For outward show an image seemingly

Within the depths of flooding river; thrust
It then much deeper still (as every gull
Gained height) until reflections disappeared
Beneath the shoreline where the watchers stood.

The man glanced sideways at his friend, toward
The cope of sky, and back down at his feet.
The gulls had gone and would not soon be seen.
"The river's pretty high," he said and turned
And started up the pathway through the trees.
His mute companion followed then but paused
To glimpse again the flooded meadowlands,
The misty hills, and April's modest green.

"flooded meadows were before them then"

"the sweep of water through the trees"

"misty hills, and April's modest green"

May

"While we sit…in the depths of the woods…, confessing the influence of almost the first summer warmth, the wood thrush sings steadily for half an hour."

~ May 28, 1855 (*Journal,* VII, 394)

In Concord Woods

Without,
The aspen and pine grove
Beats back the sun with every leaf:
A burning bush of May-green flame,
Shimmering in the heat.

Within,
The settled stillness
Of the soft, leaf-filtered light
Forms caverns of green dusk,
Dim corridors where coolness lurks:
A pillared refuge scented
With blue violets and twining honeysuckle.

Ah! here,
Here I will sit
Within these velvet woods
And lose myself in ageless dreams;
Content to count anemones
Among the last year's leaves,
Content to see upon some bare, low-hanging bough
A single wood thrush sing ethereally,
A kindred spirit in a sovereign solitude.

"beats back the sun with every leaf"

"the soft, leaf-filtered light"

"a pillared refuge"

"within these velvet woods"

Conclusion

"*The phenomena of the year take place every day....*"

(*Walden*, II, 332)

"*When the first light dawned on the earth, and the birds awoke,...all men...were invited to unattempted adventures*"; "*...as if we could be satisfied with the dews of the morning or evening without their colors, or the heavens without their azure*"; "*...we shall sooner overtake the dawn by remaining here than by hurrying over the hills of the west.*"

(*A Week on the Concord and Merrimack Rivers*, I, 121, 106, 133)

The Richer Life

Mornings, dim, white with mist: a pendant leaf
Now motionless in the expectancy
Of some great wonder to occur; then light
Flung wide in shifting curtains; staring sheep;
A cow-bell tonking somewhere; earth made new.

Afternoons, hazy, still: a soaring hawk
In trackless spiral mid the drifting clouds;
Immeasurable space; below, the far
Horizons shimmering in the heat; trees of
Dark foliage and leafy, scented shade.

Evenings, mellow with fading light: damp smells
Exuding from the earth; the upper world
Of muted crimsons, saffrons, mauves suffused
Into the blue; a newly risen moon;
I, standing, silent, listening, alone.

Then treading moon-washed roads made smooth with night's
Denial of clear vision, and stopping
Within the warm, sweet moat of air which hugs
A bush, I think of hearth and home, of dear
Tomorrow and another day to dawn.

"motionless in ... expectancy"

"dark foliage and leafy, scented shade"

"and another day to dawn"

"I have travelled a good deal in Concord." (*Walden*, II, 4)

"I would rather sit on a pumpkin and have it all to myself, than be crowded on a velvet cushion." (*Walden*, II, 41)

"…a taste for the beautiful is most cultivated out of doors." (*Walden*, II, 42)

"Simplify, simplify." (*Walden*, II, 102)

"It is a vulgar error to suppose that you have tasted huckleberries who never plucked them." (*Walden*, II, 192)

"That man is richest whose pleasures are the cheapest." (*Journal*, VIII, 205)

"I love to see anything that implies a simple mode of life and a greater nearness to the earth." (*Journal*, XIV, 88)

"When I hear a robin sing at sunset, I cannot help contrasting the equanimity of Nature with the bustle and impatience of man." (*Journal*, I, 252)

"Each town should have a park, or rather a primitive forest,…a common possession forever, for instruction and recreation." (*Journal*, XII, 387)

"I love best to have each thing in its season only, and enjoy doing without it at all other times." (*Journal*, IX, 160)

"What is the use of a house if you haven't got a tolerable planet to put it on?" (*Familiar Letters*, VI, 360)